The Heart of Pope Francis

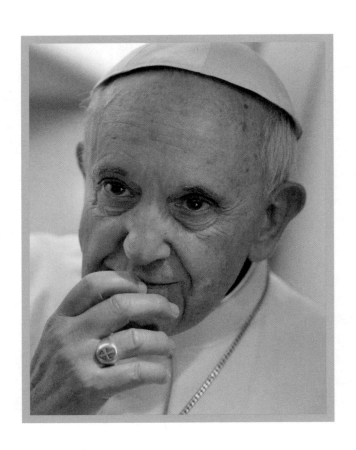

The Heart of Pope Francis

How a New Culture of Encounter
Is Changing the Church and the World

With a Foreword by Antonio Spadaro, S.J.

DIEGO FARES, S.J.

Translated by
Robert H. Hopcke

A Herder & Herder Book

THE POPE FRANCIS RESOURCE LIBRARY

The Crossroad Publishing Company
www.CrossroadPublishing.com

English translation copyright 2015
by The Crossroad Publishing Company
A Herder&Herder Book
The Crossroad Publishing Company, New York

The Heart of Pope Francis is a translation of a book originally published as
Papa Francesco è come un bambù:
Alle radici della cultura dell'incontro
© 2014 Àncora S.r.l.

The stylized crossed letter C logo is a registered trademark of
The Crossroad Publishing Company.

ISBN 978-0-8245-2074-8 (alk. paper)
Library of Congress Cataloging-in-Publication Data
available from the Library of Congress.

Cover design by George Foster
Book design by The HK Scriptorium, Inc.

In continuation of our 200-year tradition of independent publishing, The Crossroad Publishing Company proudly offers a variety of books with strong, original voices and diverse perspectives. The viewpoints expressed in our books are not necessarily those of The Crossroad Publishing Company, any of its imprints or of its employees. No claims are made or responsibility assumed for any health or other benefit.

Books published by The Crossroad Publishing Company may be purchased at special quantity discount rates for classes and institutional use. For information, please e-mail sales@CrossroadPublishing.com.

Printed in the United States of America in 2015

Contents

Preface

by Antonio Spadaro

Friendship Is Born in a Moment

On Monday, July 22, 2013, Pope Francis was flying from Rome to Rio de Janeiro to participate in the World Youth Day. During the flight, a young journalist who was with him was discussing with the Pope the situation of his own generation, particularly the level of unemployment they were suffering from and the lack of opportunity. Pope Francis suggested that the young man read "the books of Father Fares, an Argentinian Jesuit." His friend Fares's name also came off-record during an interview I did with him for *La Civià Cattolica* in August 2013.

Bergoglio has a great talent for establishing rapport with people who find him clear, direct, sincere, intense, and loyal. This is a Pope who chats on the phone with his friends, as just a part of the normal life he lives out within the course of his ministry. Of course, these days, everyone is wondering who he is as a person and how he thinks, and, in many ways, he has raised our expectations only to exceed them. But he also is a man who raises questions and issues.

Who is Jorge Mario Bergoglio? What does he think? When I interviewed him for *La Civltà Cattolica* and other Jesuit publications, I didn't think I was going to ask him this simple question, and yet I found myself asking it, spontaneously, from the heart. The answer he gave, and the way he gave it to me, struck me and gave me some insight into the person I was spending the day with, but I also got the sense that the answer I got was the very same answer he gives to his dearest friends.

That is why I turned to my fellow Jesuit Diego Fares, for I know he is one of those friends with whom Francis has shared a great deal. When I asked him to write about Francis for the journal that I edit, I confess that I wanted to start a conversation with Francis, in a way, by proxy. That conversation did eventually bear fruit, specifically in the form of this book, and its publication here has a single objective: to help people to become better and more intimately acquainted with one of Francis's fundamental notions, that of encounter.

Diego Fares's background is well suited to this task. We might call him an "intellectual," but his background is not that of the typical middle-class academic intellectual we generally imagine. With a degree in philosophy, he is a Professor of Metaphysics at the Jesuit Universidad del Salvador and at the Pontificia Universidad Católica Argentina. But he also has worked as part of a team of a hundred laypeople at St. Joseph's House (*El Hogar de San José*), a shelter for poor and homeless adults. Together with Jesuit Father Ángel Rossi, he manages Kindness House (*Casa de la Bondad*), a hospice for the terminally ill. His background is that of an intellectual who lives in the world outside the classroom and who has honed his thought through direct contact with reality on the margins of society.

He was accepted into the Society of Jesus by the then Jesuit Provincial of Argentina, Jorge Mario Bergoglio, first in September 1975 for his prenovitiate and then into the novitiate on February 21, 1976. Pope Francis was also his sponsor for priestly ordination. "I remember," says Father Fares, "that the first conversation I had with Jorge took place in the seat of the Provincial Curia, an old colonial palace, in the Flores neighborhood of the city. I was coming from Mendoza, where I was working with the Jesuits in a very poor area of town, and my first impression of the Provincial's office was one of wealth, furnished as it was with antiques and a beautiful library. What I was thinking about all this luxury must have been visible on my face in some way, because before leaving to go back to the novitiate, Jorge told me to grab my jacket and come with him. We went up to the rooftop, and there he showed me where he lived: one of those little utility rooms that you find up there, you know, where you generally store the brooms and cleaning rags. That day was a little chilly, and I got the definite impression that the door to his room did very little to keep out the cold. From that point on, my feelings and opinion of Jorge—the integrity with which he lives what he preaches—have never changed. As Péguy has said, "Friendship is born in a moment."

Bergoglio was thus his rector and director of formation at the Colegio Máximo de San José, and continued afterward as his spiritual director. "From the time I was young, he has been my guide through the Spiritual Exercises of St. Ignatius, and he taught me how to conduct the formation of young people, intellectually and spiritually." In particular, Fares thinks Bergoglio's attitude toward the poor serves as an example for his entire generation: he has shared with all around him his own enthusiasm for working with the humblest in society, and he has been tireless in constantly seeking new ways to teach and assist those in need, at all times honoring their dignity and humanity through his service.

Jorge and Diego have been friends for nearly forty years, so what follows here is one glimpse deep into the heart of a friendship and into a way of thinking that for Francis has grown over time, shaped by a lifetime of encounters, both spiritual and intellectual, that he has had with others, as well as by way of his ministry and social action.

In a recent interview, when asked to comment on the current moment we are living in the history of the Church, Diego Fares said,

> The arrival of Francis is a time of consolation for people, and not just those in the Church but for the whole world. This is what St. Ignatius called it, consolation: an increase in hope, faith, and charity, an interior joy that comforts, soothes, and quiets the soul in its Creator and

Lord. Consolation is a grace. Our Pope lives this grace personally. He has "put on the peace of the Holy Spirit," as a bishop friend of his said, and he communicates this peace to whoever is open to receiving it. We hope that as a Church we will know how to receive this peace from him and how to pass it on to the world through works of justice and mercy.

By reading the following pages, we will take a journey through Bergoglio's thought, we will touch upon the roots of this thought—in his life and intellect—and we will consider the fruits that his particular vision of a "culture of encounter" can bring to the world. One might say that Fares here has begun to sketch out the foundation for a Bergoglian political anthropology, first by examining the roots of Bergoglio the Jesuit in Chapters 1 through 3, particularly the writings of Romano Guardini, but also Dostoyevsky and contemporary Jesuit thought, then by Bergoglio the archbishop of Buenos Aires in Chapter 4, and then finally, of course, Bergoglio as Pope Francis in Chapters 5 through 7.

Fares's approach throughout, however, is personal, not dogmatic, and he interweaves his survey of Francis's thought with observations of his personality, which often reveal previously unappreciated aspects of this Pontiff and give us a deeper understanding of who he is. Fares's image of the "bamboo Pope," as well as Francis's "shoe-leather and church-bell thought," will stay with the reader as memorable ways to think about the Pope in his life and in his ministry.

The Heart of Pope Francis

ONE

"We must go out of ourselves"

OUR BELOVED FRANCIS, by the grace received in virtue of his ministry, has awakened in the Lord's faithful people hope in the God of mercy and in the father of our Lord Jesus Christ. This grace is an "active" grace that spurs us all to move, to go forward toward encountering God himself and our fellow human beings, beginning with those most in need, the marginalized.

This action of the Spirit, which in everything seeks the common good,[1] inspires us to listen to Francis, who exhorts us to keep our eyes wide open so that we might witness the miracles God has brought about among his people. He inspires us all further to help one another discover that which God—through Francis—has to say to each one of us personally, both as Church and as a people.

To speak personally, authentically, and directly is one of Francis's most striking characteristics. Every day, in his homilies, in his Wednesday audiences, in the Angelus, in the Mass, and even by way of Twitter, he speaks directly to us, because to meet us where we are is something truly and deeply dear to his heart. So open has he been about himself, particularly in the course of his present ministry, that whether with a journalist who was writing a biography of the Pope or with a doctoral student writing his dissertation about him, I myself have often had to apologize for not being able to be especially useful in providing any more information or stories or items of interests about Francis that he himself has not, in one place or another, already disclosed.

Hans Urs von Balthasar, one of Francis's favorite authors, places the study of aesthetics and theodramatics before the study of logic. In the same spirit, therefore, exploring the Pope's thinking ought not to be undertaken in order to classify or systematize his thought but rather is best used as a way to "wonder about" him, to awaken our spiritual sense about the meaning of what he says and does. Further, we would do well to loyally and unconditionally accept his invitation to experience for ourselves what he calls the two "transcendences," two ways we "go beyond ourselves": the first, in our encounter with the Father, through adoration; the second, through the encounter with our neighbor, starting first with the neediest around us, in service to them with the help of the crucified Christ.

> But ask yourselves this question: how often is Jesus inside and knocking at the door to be let out, to come out? And we do not let him out because of our own need for security, because so often we are locked into ephemeral structures that serve solely to make us slaves and not free children of God. *In this "stepping out" it is*

important to be ready for encounter. For me this word is very important. Encounter with others. Why? Because *faith is an encounter with Jesus,* and we must do what Jesus does: *encounter others.* We live in a culture of conflict, a culture of fragmentation, a culture in which I throw away what is of no use to me, a culture of waste. Yet on this point, I ask you to think—and it is part of the crisis—of the elderly, who are the wisdom of a people, think of the children . . . the culture of waste! However, we must go out to meet them, and with our faith we must create a *"culture of encounter," a culture of friendship, a culture in which we find brothers and sisters,* in which we can also speak with those who think differently, as well as those who hold other beliefs, who do not have the same faith. They all have something in common with us: they are images of God; they are children of God. Going out to meet everyone, without losing sight of our own position. There is another important point: encountering the poor. If we step outside ourselves we find poverty. Today—it sickens the heart to say so—the discovery of a tramp who has died of the cold is not news. Today what counts as news is, maybe, a scandal. A scandal: ah, that is news!²

In these words just quoted, we hear ringing in unison the principal themes of a Bergoglian culture of encounter, put into everyday language: we must go out of ourselves, because Jesus seeks to go out from the Church into the world; a culture created through faith; dialogue and diversity; the poorest among us; a society in which the death of someone living at the *Hogar de San José*[3] makes the news rather than celebrity scandals in the tabloids. These are, of course, perennial themes, but they sound new to our ears because of the spontaneous way Francis lives them and speaks about them.

López Quintás,[4] in his introduction to "Popular Opposition," tells how in one of his little-known works, in a passage about youth, Guardini talks about the way in which certain phenomena are made banal. He used the example of a church bell.

> Thus, for example, we might say that the sound of a church bell is something pure and simple, and yet at the same time rich, and that it is in both these things that its power to instill peace resides. Nothing could be more true. But is the sound of a church bell actually something simple? Those with refined hearing tell us that the most impressive bells are precisely those that display a range of complementary tones. Their sound, therefore, is not at all simple: in reality, it is, instead, a chord. A truly simple ringing would actually sound strident and hollow to our hearing. Which brings us to something important, namely: the things of the real world are always—to continue with the musical analogy—polyphonic. Only artificial things, made by man, are "simple." Living things are always born from the collaboration of various forces. They are polyphonic, complex. Which is why they have power and reality. In each of them, in some way, rings the sound of all things.[5]

The voice of Pope Francis rings with the sound of a great church bell. At the beatification of Brochero[6] in September 2013, he gave us a bell that "he made ring" in blessing it. Let us allow him to gather us up to himself, recognizing in his voice that of the Good Shepherd, who like us (and as was inscribed in the bell) "smells of his sheep."

Two

Encountering the Other

I AM VERY FAMILIAR with the admiration Pope Francis has for Romano Guardini,[1] and the notion of "encounter" this theologian put forward is well suited to what Francis wishes to get across to us when he uses this category of experience. For an interpersonal encounter to be authentic, freedom, respect, a proper perspective, esteem for the other, and dialogue must all come into play. One of Guardini's definitions summarizes all these aspects together and has a touching effect: we truly encounter another when "I am wounded by the brilliance of his being, when I am touched by his action."[2]

This is what Pope Francis is encouraging when, for example, he speaks of charitable giving, a gesture that is an authentic encounter only when we look into the eyes of the person we are helping, touching his hands, exchanging words. "If I simply toss him some coins . . . if I have not actually touched him, I have not encountered him."[3]

All of Francis's mysticism, from this perspective, can be found perhaps best expressed in his course on the Exercises, "Our Flesh in Prayer," preached at La Plata in January 1990. At that time, he said, "To draw very close to all suffering flesh is to open one's heart, to 'feel it in the gut,' to touch the wound, to carry the wounded on our backs. It is to pay the innkeeper two denarii and to guarantee even more, if it is needed. On this we will be judged." This is the reason that "the Word made flesh redeems our sinfulness, by way of suffering the passion, that is, by taking on the pain of all flesh. Jesus draws very close to all who suffer; he pays the price with his own body. Jesus does not 'pass by.' We will be judged by how closely we draw near to all who suffer, on how we treat others as our 'neighbor.'"[4]

Francis's very conception of prayer contains this notion of "touch." "Prayer touches our flesh in its very nucleus; it touches our heart." And from prayer thus described, he draws the meaning of a true "encounter," which holds those dimensions of transcendence mentioned earlier: going out of oneself to encounter God in prayer and to encounter our neighbor in service.

From an anthropological point of view, encounter is primary because it is our most human characteristic. "We are beings of encounter," beings who live out our lives in a way that cannot be denied or ignored. "Relationship is fulfilled when the other person 'encounters' (who?) the real me."[5]

Expressed affirmatively, we encounter one another through our "capacity to resonate with" others and with all things, which is why an encounter unleashes creative realities. In an encounter, there is synergy, as we say nowadays. And when an authentic encounter does not take place, our soul and our bodies are weakened and may even grow ill.

In this light, Guardini speaks of illnesses of the soul. The soul stands in relationship to the absolute values of truth, goodness, and justice, values that transcend the world of utility. If our soul loses touch with these values, in the end it grows ill.

Our soul's most basic relationship is with the truth. If we lose touch with the truth, our mind loses openness to reflect on itself, which then in turn damages our capacity to love what is good and what is right. "This does not happen when the soul merely stumbles and makes a mistake, because if it did, we would all be sick people, since we all make mistakes. Nor does it happen when we lie, even when we lie frequently. Illness of the soul only happens when it loses its basic relationship to the truth itself. When our soul loses *its will to seek the truth and the responsibilities that the truth imposes* and renounces any distinction between truth and falsehood, that is when our soul grows ill."[6] For this reason, the Pope exhorts us to "go out of ourselves to encounter the other."[7] Indeed, he admits that whoever goes out and opens himself up to the world may well have an unpleasant collision, but Francis insists that he would rather have a Church that collides with the world than an ailing Church that remains shut up in its sacristy. From here, too, comes his oft-repeated, indefatigable assurance to us that God never tires of forgiving; thus his recommendation that in the sacrament of reconciliation we be as clear as possible as we confess our sins: "I did this, and this, and this."

Clearly, we see that his counsel on these points does not come from a purely moral set of values but arises from an existential discernment in which what is at stake is our spiritual (and physical) health. In going outside ourselves toward what can be discovered in a genuine encounter with an other (if with God, a confession of the truth of sinful nature; if neighbor, beginning with the neediest), what is at stake is our relationship to Truth, Love, and Justice. Without authentic encounter, we limit ourselves to merely self-referential, utilitarian, or purely functional relationships, or worse still, relationships of exclusion or domination, in which we not only hurt others but we make ourselves sick as well, as when we say someone is "insane with power" or "drunk with pride." These are not mere figures of speech but literal, spiritual truths.

By contrast, let us consider how Guardini describes a "man of encounter." He says, "When a man is at his most vital, when his relationship to the world is at its most fresh, he then *lives his life through encounter* and retains his capacity to encounter the other even through old age."[8] "The reverse of this capacity," Guardini adds, "is habit, indifference, snobbishness." These last qualities could not be further from the personality of Pope Francis, who, by letting himself be touched by God's newness, gives everyone a personal embrace and shows a simplicity and humility about him that is the very antithesis of snobbishness.

The Pope has said that it is a grace, in his current ministry, to be able to "draw near to people first, and then only later on worry about the problems of the Vatican." In writing to Eugenio Scalfari, he himself defines his faith:

Faith, for me, is born of an encounter with Jesus. A personal encounter that has touched my heart, given me a direction and a new sense of my existence.[9] But at the same time an encounter that was made possible by the faith community in which I have lived and thanks to whom I have had access to the wisdom of Holy Scripture, to the new life that like sparkling water flows from Jesus through the sacraments, to fellowship with all people and to service to the poor, the true images of the Lord. Without the Church, I believe, I would not have been able to encounter Jesus, aware as I am of how that enormous gift that is our faith must be carried in the fragile clay vessels of our humanity. So, it is precisely from my personal experience of a faith lived in the Church that I find myself able to listen to what it asks of me and to seek, with the whole Church, the roads on which we all might begin to walk down together.[10]

This brief introduction to Romano Guardini and the passages quoted here from his writings on the Gospel should be enough to show how it has been a touchstone for the Pope's words and deeds throughout his ministry. Inspired by them, his life shows him successful at finding that source of living water beneath the desert of modern life. His direct and authentic encounters with all people are such that they "have life and have it abundantly." This, in Guardini's words, is love.

In his relationship to the truth of his faith, Francis is not a man who "for fear of making a mistake says nothing at all," but on the contrary, is someone who never renounces the truth of God's love for every person. He does not refrain from speaking, even if what he says at times is taken out of context or viewed abstractly such that he ends up being misinterpreted by the scribes and Pharisees of our day. With Francis, though, one can be certain that the conversation, whatever the topic, will be authentic, sincere, and fruitful.

THREE

"God's faithful people are infallible"

F RANCIS'S PREACHING aims to create a "culture of encounter," a long-standing notion of his that is united to his idea of a "faithful people." To be clear, when he uses the word "culture," he is not talking about "refined" or "polite" people, "cultured" in the intellectual sense. Such connotations come from our own ideas of the way in which culture is conflated with sophistication, or intellectualism, or a refinement of taste.

The Religious Resource That People of Faith Possess

As early as 1974, the then-quite-young Provincial Jorge Bergoglio, at the opening of the Provincial Conference of Argentinian Jesuits, pointed out the need to recognize "the religious resource that people of faith possess,"[1] and he went on to say that "for me, they are the most important part, the most real: people of faith."

To begin with, the first thing he did was to "enlarge the category." "When I say, 'people of faith,' I am speaking indeed simply about faithful people," adding, "those with whom we have most contact in our own priestly ministries and in our religious witness." The images in Bergoglio's mind here are those humble people of faith making a pilgrimage to the Shrine of Luján,[2] where, each year as archbishop, he spent the night taking the confessions of those on the road; people of faith expressing their love at the Shrine of Our Lord of the Miracle at Salta[3]; and finally those people of faith from the *barrio* of Los Polvorines, where, as a student, Francis was a missionary, or at the parish of Patriarca San Giuseppe, where he served as the first pastor.

Second, Bergoglio leaves behind any "ideological pre-suppositions." "Obviously, the term 'people' is, for us, a vague term depending upon which ideological presuppositions one uses to define the reality of a 'people.'" So he emphasizes, "I mean quite simply faithful people."[4]

Third, he defines the term "narratively":

> When I studied theology, when, like you all, I was combing through Denzinger's *Sources of Catholic Dogma* and various other treatises in order to defend my thesis, one traditional Christian formulation struck me: the faithful people of God are infallible *in credendo*, in their belief. It is from this insight that I drew my own personal formulation, which is less precise but which I have found helpful nevertheless: when you wish to know what our Holy Mother Church believes, turn to the Magisterium, for it has the charge of teaching what we believe without error; but if you wish to know what the Church believes, turn to the faithful people of God.

Thus, his definition for the term "people of faith" is phe-nomenological and is drawn from their action, from their expressions of love for Mary, the way they emulate "how she loves."[5] To this Bergoglio adds, "Our people possess a soul, and since we can speak of the soul of a people, we can likewise speak of a hermeneutic, a way of seeing real-ity, a consciousness of one's own dignity ... a conscience formed through meaningful experience and not simply as the product of a theory, from a life that is, at its root, Christian."[6]

The Tragedy of Splitting Gospel and Culture

In 1975, *Evangelii nuntiandi* of Paul VI was published, and the 32nd General Congregation of the Jesuits took place. Bergoglio has always considered *Evangelii nuntiandi* as a particularly inspired document. In it, Paul VI stated that "the split between the Gospel and culture is without a doubt the drama of our time, just as it was of other times. Therefore, every effort must be made to ensure a full evan-gelization of culture, or more correctly, of cultures. They have to be regenerated by an encounter with the Gospel."[7]

In an article entitled "Criteria for Apostolic Action," which was based on the Acts he compiled of the preced-ing meeting of Jesuit superiors (May 2-3, 1979) over which he presided as Provincial, Bergoglio spoke of the people as "a resource" and said that the "inculturation of the Gos-pel," which has at its aim "a process of structural change (including the structure of one's own heart), must accomplish the task of providing justice so as to avoid betraying the culture, values, and legitimate aspirations of our people, and likewise, to avoid seeing them through the lens of our 'enlightened' mentality."[8] He went on, "It is the people who carry history forward, and the Church must influence them if their culture is to be evangelized. The incarnation of the Gospel demands that Christ be proclaimed and welcomed in different ways in different countries and in different environments, acknowledging the richness in each of them. Because inculturation, from a universal point of view and yet one which has valid application to a variety of situations, means diversity (of culture, function, and modality) within conceptual unity."[9]

Other characteristics of God's faithful people can be seen in everyday life: "People have habits, values, cultural artifacts that evade any neat classification: they are empowered to question." And this empowerment means:

> We must listen carefully to the subtleties, adopting an attitude of humility, affection, adapting to the culture and especially rejecting on its face the absurd idea of giving "voice" to a people, as if they had none of their own. All peoples have a voice, even it has been reduced by oppression to a whisper. We must sharpen our hearing and listen to that voice, and not speak in their place. As a pastor, the first question to be asked in the face of any structural change should be, "What does my people want? What are they calling me to?" And we must have the courage to listen and to do so without losing sight of the broader horizon of history.[10]

So, when Pope Francis speaks of "culture," he is speaking about the "soul of a people," its voice, which is at times reduced by oppression to a mere whisper. He also speaks of a people's awareness of its own dignity, as indicated by the important events of its history, its way of loving God, and its empowerment, in particular its power to question those with whom it dialogues.

The Inculturation of the Gospel

The best-known decree of the 32nd General Congregation of Jesuits is the fourth, entitled "Our Mission Today: Deacons of Faith, Promotion of Justice." Bergoglio has consistently emphasized that for him the most inspired part of this text was not the polemic between faith and justice but the passages about inculturation, and with the passage of time, his intuition on this point has proven on target. "In recent years a growing conviction has been establishing itself more and more firmly in the conscience of the Society; our mission to serve the faith by promoting justice is widening toward a transformative dialogue with different cultures and different religions." At that time, his comments about Decree #4—used as a banner by those who would champion the cause of the poor even to the point of taking up arms and, conversely, used as a warning by those opposed to such action on behalf of the poor—definitely emphasized this struggle for justice and remained faithful to the beauty expressed in Paragraph 50. As Bergoglio said,

By walking patiently and humbly with the poor, we will discover how we may help them, after first having welcomed them. Without this slow, patient walk alongside them, any action we might take on behalf of the poor and oppressed is contrary to our intention and instead *we will impede them from fully feeling their own aspirations and from acquiring those tools they need to effectively assume responsibility for their own personal and collective destiny.* Through humble service, we have the opportunity to lead them toward discovering, through the heart of their difficulties and struggles, the living Jesus Christ working in the power of the Holy Spirit. We can then speak to them of God the Father, who reconciles humanity to himself and establishes among all people a community of brotherhood.[11]

We might say that Bergoglio intuited the way in which the requirement of justice was (and still is) one of the "questions" the people of God are empowered to pose.

And that is not the only question: Paul VI asked the Society to "confront the multiple forms of contemporary atheism," one form of which—structural injustice—represents a kind of atheism in practice; but it is certainly not the only form, for it is a kind of atheism when the "voiceless poor are considered solely from a sociological point of view" or come to be subjected to the reductionist Marxist perspective.

Faithful to the spirit of Decree #4, as edited and approved *in toto*, Bergoglio developed his notion of formation, which he put into practice in the poor neighborhoods of San Miguel, where his contact with "popular culture and piety" allowed him "to be educated little by little" and to learn to listen to the questions that the faithful people of God were asking in their lives. This is how Bergoglio was able to go beyond the false dichotomy of progressive and conservative that divided—and still divides—the Church.

Solidarity Unites the Collective with the Individual

In 1989, Bergoglio gave the first lecture of the academic year at San Miguel; his topic: "The Need for Political Anthropology: A Pastoral Problem."[12] In his talk, he sketched out the basis for answering the following question: "On what sort of political anthropology should one base the proclamation of the Gospel?" To speak of a political anthropology implies "the right approach to the values of the times,"[13] and here Bergoglio adopts Guardini's criteria, looking at the relationship between the fullness of human potential and the real concrete opportunities offered to people of our time. This simple comparison, applicable to any situation, explains why we see an increase in tension, suffering, and violence being manifested in our cultures. We all see the inequality with which the resources on which we all rely are being consumed, and this inequality indicates "a lack of governance," a lack of control on the part of government. Such inequality is "the implicit expression of all that is uncivil." Government, which ensures civilization, has now become a faceless entity, for which no one assumes responsibility, creating the current situation in which "we are cast back into the dark abyss of primitive times, the anguish of the wilderness, the horror of darkness. Human beings find themselves once again standing before chaos."[14]

Bergoglio proposes *solidarity* as the attitude and the value that, when deeply established, can salvage this situation and foster a change in political attitudes that will in turn overcome the false dichotomies of the present time in a real and effective way. Solidarity "unites the collective (a source of undeniable power) with the individual (the uniqueness of the human person, expressed in the ethics of responsibility and loyalty, possessing an ontological openness to the transcendent reality of others and of God). Solidarity is the way history is made; solidarity is the living environment where conflicts, tension, and opposites come together into a life-giving unity of many forms."[15] And further he states, "If nowadays we see a postmodern humanity submerged in the confused disillusionment of their failed omnipotence, we can find no other form of rescue save that of re-encounter, a joining back with one's own people, united by the bond of yearning for God who is the Beginning and the End of their freedom of action."[16] A culture of encounter, therefore, brings together with a kind of natural resonance the category of culture with that of the people such that when one says, "cultures and peoples," plural, the emphasis is placed on respect for and attention to differences, without which true unity remains an abstraction, rather than a concrete, lived reality.

What does it mean to bring together cultures and peoples? A number of things, but the first is that any genuine interpersonal encounter must occur within the context of a people. From the Christian point of view, it is clear that such genuine interpersonal encounters occur in the midst of the Church, which is the people of God. Bergoglio's idea is that "one can take Guardini's ecclesial vision—wherein a person is a participant insofar as he or she belongs to Catholic time and space—and transpose it onto a vision of a people, indeed, every people, where it would have a similar character."[17] He similarly notes that "to share the collective consciousness of a people is to let oneself enter into a unique reciprocity of mutual benefit, to allow oneself to be enlightened by the piety with which that same people is moved to strive, which is its justification, which is its hope, which gives it its joy for life."[18]

Behind this conception of "people" we find once more Guardini, and behind him, Dostoyevsky and *The Brothers Karamazov*:

> It is the people who, despite their misery and sinfulness, are authentically human, and despite their abjection, are rich and healthy, because their roots are sunk deep in the essential structure of being. . . . Who does not believe in God does not believe either in the people

of God. But whoever believes in the people of God reflects upon His holiness, even if he never believed in it before.

From an anthropological perspective, this conception of peoples and cultures goes beyond those random and fragmentary "abstract" relationships that globalization proposes or imposes on us, wherein freedom is understood merely as a function of consumerist logic. It is a conception that also gives rise to many points of reflection and debate. "To listen" to the people, even the word "people" itself carries a cost. It always "makes noise." Not so with other words. "Citizen,'" for example, seems less ideological, more neutral, more politically correct. Indeed, the more abstract the words, the less conflict they create. They are neither virus nor vitamin, as Bergoglio might say. Back when he was archbishop of Buenos Aires, he explained, "One can only use the word 'people' if one takes responsibility, if one participates. It is more than a word. It is a call, it is a summons to go out from oneself."[19]

Archbishop Victor Manuel Fernandez[20] also said it well. When asked, "What does the theology of the people mean? And why does Francis have a twinkle in his eye when he says the word 'people,'" his answer was:

A theology of the people is as distinct from Marxist analyses as it is from the positions of liberals. Neither of these perspectives is relevant to it. It rather means considering the poor not just as mere objects to be liberated or educated but rather as subjects who are capable of thinking in their own ways, capable of living out their own faith with legitimacy in their own way, capable of moving forward on the basis of the culture of their own people. A "people" is not the same as "the masses," because the expression "people" presumes a collective subject that is able to generate its own historic process. One may add to this, but always with respect for identity and style.[21]

FOUR

Encountering Jorge Bergoglio

A T THIS POINT, it is necessary to draw attention to
our method here, essentially, a chronological review
of texts that address the "culture of encounter." Since Bergoglio's writings are not especially numerous, from the
practical point of view, it would seem we have an easy job
ahead of us. But his statements, since having been elected
Pope, have grown in number in a surprising way, and the
relationship between all of these statements has therefore
become more complex.

By making use of Guardini's phenomenological abil-
ity to "see living figures,"[1] to see a whole that is fraught
with dynamic tension among its parts, Pope Francis gives
coherence to his various statements. But it is really out of
the matrix of Ignatian discernment that his often-spoken
words are offered now within an even more vital context of grace and *consolation*, lending them new life and
depth. The work he carried out throughout all the countless encounters he had during his time as an archbishop

doing his pastoral duty reveals a rich network of "inculturated" roots he has put down within the concrete reality of our country, Argentina, and these roots have borne fruit a hundredfold.

Consolation may well be the key word. When a work has been done for God, with dedication and love, patiently kneaded into the monotony of one's daily routine, when the grace of consolation finally comes, it shines in all its splendor. I would like to say that whatever happens due to the Pope's actions also happens by way of the Pope's writings. Those worn black shoes of his that walked the streets of Buenos Aires, shoes no one thought very special in themselves, now seem to shine with far more brilliance than any pair of symbolic red shoes he may be wearing now as Pope.

During his days as archbishop of Buenos Aires, three moments are, to my mind, especially significant.

In the Face of Fragmentation

One does well, first, to recall the moment when he delineated for the first time his notion of a "culture of encounter" *per se,* in 1999, during the *Te Deum* on May 25. At that time, he recommended that we "let our thirst for encounter grow" as an antidote for nostalgia and pessimism. Some months later, while speaking to teachers, his topic was specifically "Education within a Culture of Encounter," and on that occasion, Cardinal Bergoglio once again took up and expanded on ideas he had first presented in "The Need for a Political Anthropology" in 1989, this time recasting them in terms of encounter. "I would like to offer a proposal: we need to generate a culture of encounter. In the face of a culture of fragmentation, as some would call it, or at the very least, a culture of nonintegration, the difficult times we face will require much more of us: we cannot rely on those who would capitalize on resentment or on our forgetting the history we share, those who enjoy weakening the ties that bind us all together."[2] The Cardinal anticipated the danger of social fragmentation that Argentina would suffer from 2001 onward.[3]

One aspect of this discussion was his invitation to

> engage in the exercise of opening up space for encounter. In contrast to a retrograde superficiality or opportunism (flowers that bear no fruit), ours is a people endowed with a collective memory that is not afraid to walk forward into the future with the nobility that characterizes it: communitarian efforts and activities, a growing number of local initiatives, so many movements of mutual aid, all these are occurring in a dynamic whirlwind of selfless participation that has rarely been seen in this country. We leaders must take action using this revitalized national bond. Empowering and protecting it may well be our principal mission.[4]

In addition, it is important to highlight Bergoglio's notion of "cultural discernment." In many of his writings, he talks of the symptoms of a cultural illness that threatens us in the very core of our soul, in our relationship with truth, goodness, and justice.

> A technical mentality along with a secular messianism are two traits seen today that we can easily qualify as "gnostic." Champions of knowledge but deprived of integration, while simultaneously hungry for the esoteric, which is in this case secularized or, as we might say, profane in nature. For this reason, we note that education nowadays tends toward the gnostic and the esoteric, since it is unable to make use of techniques of interior integration made possible by real ends achieved by real means in a human way. Moreover, this crisis cannot be overcome by any type of "return" (those incessant experiments we have seen throughout the agonies of our modern age) but will be overcome by drawing upon a superabundance within, to be found in the heart of the very crisis itself, accepting it fully for what it is but without being caught in it and instead transcending it by going inward.[5]

Discernment is a gift of the Spirit[6] and has an eminently practical character. The grace of "discerning"—separating and distinguishing—good spirits from bad is made concrete in "welcoming" the movement of the good and putting these into practice while "rejecting" those of the bad, condemning them and doing the opposite of what they suggest. The so-called "Francis effect" is one fruit of the grace of discernment long present in Bergoglio but which now, in his papal ministry, has been abundantly and unexpectedly fruitful in many ways. Having discerned the way evil spirits have made us sick through discord, fighting, and division, he has now "opened the doors" to go out and embrace in person everyone and everything that can be encountered, inspiring others to do the same as a "cure," as a balm, something we have unconsciously desired forever. And at the same time, the Pope "rejects" and "banishes" any theoretical plans or practices that lead to non-encounter. For the Pope, the "interior unity" of man "flows from a love for true ends (the well-being of actual people, beginning with one's neighbor and the neediest among us) and the use of means in a human way." In an interpersonal encounter (be it family, community, or church), true ends are reinforced, and the means for achieving them are found, quite naturally, in a human way.

The Aparecida Proposals

Second, we would like to call attention to the "Aparecida Proposals for the Clergy of the Argentinian Church" (August 15, 2009). In this work, he focuses on all the pastoral work of the preceding years, in particular, the revised, final version of the Aparecida document (May 13-31, 2007),[7] that of the 10th Day of Social Ministry, "Toward a Culture of Encounter: Politics, Mediator of the Common Good," and his examination of culture in "Parish and Family" (January 2007) and in "Culture and Popular Piety" (January 19, 2008).

Bergoglio's words emphasize that the "fullness of life proposed at Aparecida is illuminated in part by the notion of encounter." And this is for two reasons: "In the first place, because I believe it is the anthropological notion used most frequently in the document. And in the second place, because our main sin, as Argentineans, is conflict, not encounter."

From Aparecida, he says,

> Abundance of life comes through an encounter with Jesus Christ. The text of John 10:10 on abundance of life draws all the themes of Aparecida toward it like a magnet; it is their center point. In this text, the Lord defines his ministry. "I have come that you might have life and have it abundantly." The memory of the foundational encounter of our faith is at the beginning and is carried through right through to the end of the Document.[8]

Bergoglio shows how "the opposite of encounter is an *isolated conscience*, from which the encounter with Jesus Christ rescues us 'so that gratitude and joy might overflow.' An isolated conscience provokes and reinforces nonencounter. Whoever holds his conscience apart from the path of God's holy people undergoes a metamorphosis of distance, a turning inward."

He gives great importance to the "three aspects of encounter that Aparecida puts forward as contrasted with their opposites in an isolated conscience: (1) the experience of personal encounters; (2) an abundance of life that renders encounter stable and continuous, thereby bridging the generational divide; and (3) an abundance of life that requires a ministry *directed toward encounter*, to keep us from that isolated conscience created by self-referentiality, self-contentment, clericalism or elitist and exclusionary ideologies." On this last point, Aparecida places the emphasis on actions, attitudes, and processes that contribute to this "movement toward encounter," all of which give life to gratitude, inclusiveness, listening, and conversation.

Dialogue, the Most Useful Tool

Third, in Days 12 and 13 on social ministry, Cardinal Bergoglio emphasized the notions of dialogue and people. On dialogue he said,

> To foster encounter, the most useful tool is dialogue, to create the capacity for dialogue. When a person enters into an encounter, he begins to dialogue, and dialogue means not simply hearing but listening. One must foster this capacity for listening. The other person, no matter on what side of the street he happens to be ideologically, politically, or socially, always has something good to offer, just as I have something good to offer him. Through our encounter, into which I carry these good things, is built a creative, fecund synthesis. Dialogue is, fundamentally, fecundity. Monologues

produce nothing. One of the great minds of Argentina, in my opinion, one of the greatest, Santiago Kovad-loff, spoke a while back about danger, about the risk of homogenizing our words; but behind this is an even greater risk, an even more serious illness: a homogenization of thought, an autism of the intellect and of feeling that leads us to see reality from within our own bubble. Thus, it is crucial we retrieve our capacity to dialogue with others.[9]

On people:

To be full citizens, it is not enough simply to belong to society; to truly have the identity of a full citizen it is not enough—as great a step as it may be—simply to legally belong to a society. To be in a society and to be qualified as one of its citizens, in the categorical sense, is a great step forward in functionality, to be sure, but a person in society takes an even more precise identity as a citizen by belonging to a people. This is fundamental, for identity means to belong. There is no identity without belonging. The challenge of a person's identity as a citizen is in direct proportion to the way in which that person lives out this belonging. But belonging to whom? To the people in which he was born and with whom he lives. A culture of encounter succeeds by giving priority to dialogue, by sharing a search for consensus, for agreement, for all that unites us in place of all that divides or opposes us. That is the road we must travel. To do so we must give priority to time over space, to the whole over the partial, to reality as over against abstraction and to unity over conflict. [And this requires] that the protagonist be the historic subject that is the people and its culture, not a class, not a faction, not a group nor an élite. This way forward must be strategically planned. It can happen. And it is something that the people ardently desire.[10]

FIVE

The God of Pope Francis

THE LAST MENTION of a culture of encounter that Bergoglio made as cardinal was during the closing Mass at the Meeting of Urban Clergy in the Buenos Aires area:

> Our God is a God who is close. And special: he cures, he does good. Saint Peter clearly says, "He goes among us blessing and healing." Jesus did not proselytize: he walked with people. Our God is close to us. *The God of encounter who seeks to encounter his people.* The God who places his people in situations of encounter. *And by his closeness, by this accompaniment, he creates a culture of encounter* that makes us brothers, children, and not just members of an NGO or proselytes of a multinational organization. *Closeness.* That is what is proposed.[1]

And closeness was precisely what he was able to establish during his first encounter with the people as Bishop of Rome, unconditionally and personally receiving a multitude of people. With humility, he expressed gratitude for this "welcome" and spoke of starting on the road together, a flock with their shepherd. By asking people for their blessing, in a few moments he won their hearts. According to a public relations specialist, whoever told the Pope to act that way was a pure genius.

All that Father Jorge had previously lived and thought in his former ministry far from the spotlight is now being made public, is now "blossoming," in his words and deeds as Pope. We use the word "blossoming" intentionally to move away from the cliché of "how much the Papacy has changed him." In actuality, Father Jorge has not changed. What was always there has now merely "blossomed" forth on a larger world stage.

The image brought to mind is that of Japanese bamboo, which, when first planted, over the course of seven years, grows almost imperceptibly but which then, in a period of six weeks, suddenly grows 100 feet. Do we say that the bamboo grew that tall in merely six weeks? No, the truth is that it took six weeks plus seven years to grow that tall. In the first seven years of apparent inactivity, the bamboo was busy putting down that complex system of roots it needed that would then allow such sudden growth after those seven years. Few are the people who instead of wilting with age blossom forth and give the best of themselves. Pope Francis is one of these people.

What happened at the beginning of his pontificate is extraordinary. The life he had lived before came to light, and his past was re-evaluated in an extraordinary way. The richness of current events in his life is the integration of the past he has lived, and it inspires admiration particularly because the humility of his actions from before comes to light after all these years. Indeed, things have come to light about who he is and what he has done that one might have thought would never come to light, stories told by the very people involved. In fact, the Pope is the first to tell stories about his life before, and not just his success but his failures. How great a grace this is, it's hard to tell, because it is happening for us in real time.

Re-encountering Pope Francis

Pope Francis's capacity for encounter, thus, is not something we merely witness on a daily basis in St. Peter's Square—as he waves tirelessly from the popemobile or in Rio, when he humbly knocks on someone's door, asking to be let in, or in Lampedusa, when he becomes emotional while preaching—but it extends back throughout his life and thus provides for what one might best call "re-encounter." In our introductory examination of what Pope Francis means by "a culture of encounter," therefore, we do well to direct our attention to the additional idea of "re-encountering."

For us, his fellow Argentineans, our experience of Francis has been one of re-encounter. While the relationship the rest of the world has to him begins in the present and extends into the future, for us it is woven into our history. One thing in this regard that helps those of us who have known him (as happened to some of Jesus's companions, once he too became well known) is for us to truly take to heart what Francis means when he says "availability" and recommends that we let ourselves "be guided by the Spirit." When people who do not know him conjecture that he "was not always like this," we who have known him all along have to say that he is the same as he has always been: happy, cordial, smart. And why is it that some who have met him cannot understand how they missed these qualities in him? The reason here is quite simple: he was not yet Pope. To be who he is, to let himself be shaped by the ministry with which he has been entrusted, to receive a "position of grace," all these things Francis has always lived out as fully as possible; and in the end, this grace is largely due to the teachings of St. Ignatius and the Spiritual Exercises: disposing oneself to receive grace, making oneself available, embracing what the Lord has chosen for us, accepting the struggle the Lord gives us, carrying out the mission that we have been chosen for.[2]

When he was novice master, Bergoglio saw to the formation process. When elected provincial, he led.[3] When in the parish as pastor, he served the neighborhood as pastor without fuss, teaching catechism to the children, washing the feet of the elderly in St. Joseph's Parish.[4] When appointed auxiliary bishop, he assisted the bishop. When named archbishop, he served as archbishop. When asked to oversee the editing of the Aparecida document, he served as editor.[5] And now that he is Pope—he is the Pope.

It is interesting that an essential aspect of encounter is in fact re-encounter. Indeed, from a theological point of view, being a child of God means first acknowledging our sinfulness—our separation from God—such that whatever relationship with the Father we come to is always a "re-encounter," a point perhaps best illustrated in the parable of the Prodigal Son (Luke 15:11-32).

From a political point of view, the fighting that takes place within Argentinian society is so obvious and, unfortunately, commonplace that the bitter result such discord has produced cannot be avoided: our pride about claiming "our part of the inheritance," despising our brothers and sisters. Such attitudes show profound disrespect to our country, which actually says to all of us, like the father in the parable, "Children, all I have is yours." Only an appreciation of how much we have been given by our life and history in Argentina, appreciation that, like a good seed, needs to be sown, tended, and grown in the same ground as the weeds of discord and conflict, only this can uproot the pride of an oligarchic few who believe they are more important than the whole of the country and all its people.

To "re-encounter" Francis, as we all are called to do, is a unique opportunity for us: it is an occasion to deepen the meaningfulness of our relationship. Dulhalde's embrace of Menem shows us the way forward.[6]

The Music of Encounter

Having brought together and examined Francis's writings on the culture of encounter, one gets the impression that, on the one hand, he has talked about this subject for a very long time while on the other, it feels like something completely new and different. Might this be because of the context? A cab driver who was following the Spiritual Exercises in his home spoke with the Pope and said, "Nowadays it seems you priests are better are preaching," to which, Francis, a bit taken aback, replied, "Nowadays, it seems that you lay-people, too, are better at listening."

Here is an example of yet another quality of his, specifically, the tone he sets. It seems he pays less attention to the words he speaks and more to the "music." Not long ago, when speaking of "young politicians," he said,

> I find young politicians think differently about politics. Not better or worse, but simply different. They speak in a different way; they are looking for something different. Their *music* is different from ours. We are not afraid. Let us listen to them. Let us speak with them. They have an intuition; let's listen to their intuition. It is the intuition of youth. I say young politicians, because that's whom I've noticed, but young people in general are looking to live their lives in a different key. It would help our encounter with them if we listened to the music of these politicians or scientists, these young thinkers.[7]

This reference to music, indeed, comes from the Spiritual Exercises and from his experience as novice master and spiritual director.[8] As director, when one listens to what a directee engaged in the Exercises has prayed throughout the day, one does not pay attention to what the directee has thought about the Gospel but rather how the Gospel has moved him or her so as to discern the good spirits from the bad, to discern whether the person feels consolation or desolation—and this one hears through the tone, through the "music," as Francis calls it.

On this point, Joaquín García Roca's reflections on the Pope's "narrative of the heart" are very inspiring, especially when he notes how the prophetic and teaching aspects of what he says do not simply address matters of dogma but serve to broaden an overall perspective and make polyphonic what once was simply a monologue.

Pope Francis is fostering other forms of relationship with the reality around us, and he shows an appreciation for real experience—common sense, traditional stories, casual acquaintances. When an elderly woman asks for forgiveness, not only does he provide her what she asks for but he recognizes it as an example of her wisdom. In speaking of what happened during his meeting with someone who was ill, he demonstrates the importance of story in relationship. When he listens to what an immigrant has gone through, he shows us the value of listening. In this way, we find ourselves changing our perspective so that, without negating scripture, doctrine, or formal reasoning, we value instead the reasons of the heart. "I invite them to listen to their heart." "I wish to enter Brazil through the doorway of the heart." Francis is giving us the message that we do not need doctrine to find value in others.[9]

García Roca underscores here the diffractive aspect of Francis's model, which "eschews monolinguals" and pursues instead the "polyphony of reason."[10]

The conclusion we should draw from all this is clear, for when someone speaks to us this way, we cannot help but listen. The culture of encounter is not just *inter pares*, among equals—as we say—but hierarchical. It is necessary for all of us to listen to the Spirit that guides us, not just to whoever happens to speak most beautifully but to whoever is of service, to whoever gives of himself. We meet each other around the immediacy of Francis, who, by the way he listens to us, goes out from himself and grounds himself in Jesus.

With Francis, it is not simply a matter of the "music as over against the words," but also and especially a question of "timing," rhythm, as Guardini would say. By the way he chooses the exact moment to speak, to make use of the situation, he demonstrates a mastery of timing, which is a gift received through the grace of the Spirit. For if anything comes from God, it is time. It is the humble, receptive person who knows how to take advantage of the moment, the *kairos*, who is attentive to the Word, who is prompt in acting, like the Blessed Mother, like St. Joseph.

Pope Francis tells the story of when, during his flight to Rio de Janeiro, he didn't want to give interviews, because his words would be compared to what he would be saying the next day, whereas, on his flight back from Rio, he had no problem talking to reporters and was happy to speak quite openly on any topic. This is a small example of a larger quality. Indeed, in spiritual direction, he was quite capable of biding his time for many years and mentioning something important only when the person wanted to and was able to hear it and make use of it. Yet, another example of his knowing how to seize the moment is the letter that he wrote to Eugenio Scalfari in which he used the question that the journalist had asked to begin a genuine dialogue and to reflect in a new way on the topic of truth.

On this point, we recall what Guardini has said about "the relationship between illness and truth" and look at how the Pope has pursued this theme. With Scalfari, who asked about absolute truth, Francis replied,

> I would not speak, even to a believer, about "absolute" truth, since the absolute is without connection, stands outside relationship. Rather, the truth, according to the Christian faith, is God's love for us in Jesus Christ. For us, truth *is* relationship. Such that every one of us welcomes this truth and expresses it in our own way, through our history and culture, the way in which we live. This does not mean that the truth is subjective and variable. Quite the opposite. It means rather that the truth is given to each of us as a path we must follow in the life we live. Didn't Jesus say, "I am the way, the truth, and the life?" In other words, the truth, being fundamentally at one with love, requires humility of us and an openness to finding it, listening to it and expressing it. So it's important to understand the terms

we are using and to leave behind the strictures of absolute contrasts, so as to examine these questions more deeply.[11]

The Pope, in this way, has turned an "absolute contrast" into a fertile tension: the truth is given to each of us as a path we must follow in the life we live. These illustrations of how to live a culture of encounter help us to listen to and savor when and to whom Francis turns, to hear the music he is hearing within and therefore to move ourselves toward encountering one another.

Going Out to Encounter the Poor

Having noted his talent for knowing when to seize the "opportunity" (which is the key element in any encounter, after all), we can appreciate another basic aspect of encounter that Pope Francis brings to light: urgency. He urges us to "come from an encounter with the poor, with the rejected" (the *sobrantes*, as expressed in Aparecida). Francis remains consistently inspired in his thought by the refrain "Time is more important than space." The culture of encounter is a matter of time, and that which characterizes the right moment, the now, is to go out of oneself and seek those on the margins.

On May 18, 2013, on the Vigil of Pentecost (in a statement that, every time we read it, seems more and more inspired), the Pope seemed to be thinking out loud when he affirmed the necessity of going out of ourselves and "finding poverty."

> Poverty, for us Christians, is not a sociological or philosophical category: it is a theological category. I might

say, it is the *primary category*, because that God, the Son of God, came down and made himself poor so as to walk alongside us on the road. And this is our poverty: the poverty of Christ in the flesh, that poverty that brought us the Son of God in his Incarnation. A Church that is poor and that serves the poor begins by turning toward the body of Christ. *If we turn toward the body of Christ, we begin to understand,* to understand what this poverty is, the poverty of our Lord.[12]

What is it that "we begin to understand" when we move toward an encounter with the poverty of Christ in the flesh? We begin to understand the central point of Christianity, as St. Albert Hurtado has said, "the sense of poverty. I believe that is the core of Christianity."[13] We do well to pay attention to this "beginning of understanding." Listening is important. To hear a statement like "Go out and teach what you know and give away what you have treasured" is very different from hearing "Go out and encounter the poorest among you, because Christ brings the good news and blesses everyone with his love."

Why all this insistence on going out? During his course on the Exercises in 1990, in a meditation entitled "The Exile of All Flesh: The Prayer of the Exiled Body," Bergoglio reflected on how "our body feels the exile imposed upon it." The banishment of Adam from the Garden; the exile of the people of Israel, deported over and over again; the exile of our Lord, stripped of everything, abandoned by God and man. Whoever "goes out of oneself" and takes on the exile "follows the path of singular purification."

Prayer is the privileged place of exile. That is where one is given revelation (here is the beginning of understanding), that is, passing from what one thinks about God to that which God truly is. . . . The exile of all flesh, the experience of homelessness, without father or mother, without even a dog to welcome us; the exile from one's self (since no one is at peace in one's own heart; there is always conflict); the exile from men and from God (since all is silence), all these give rise to the deepest conversations in our flesh. It is a wound that then is "tended" and "touched" by God.[14]

We see how this "going toward an encounter with the wounded body of Christ" reveals the authentic image of God in Jesus Christ and how we then are "touched" by his mercy. The "exiled" of this world, the rejected, are not primarily "objects of a duty to be accomplished" but people in whose fragility we are able to "recognize that same image in a mixture of earth and treasure."[15] And in this encounter, "compassion becomes communion." The theological depth of the Pope's prayer here is an important contribution, though of course we might well say that such reflections were already a part of Decree 4 of the 32nd General Congregation of the Jesuits where a "preferential option for the poor" and the "promotion of justice" were described as always taking place within the context of an encounter, by walking alongside the other, listening, and learning.

From all of the above comes Francis's "triple perspective," as García Roca puts it:

In the first place, he proposes a perspective of concrete realization, rather than abstract, idealistic, or rhetorical approximations, because he says quite frankly, "a theoretical poverty is no use to us. Poverty is learned by touching the flesh of the poor Christ, in the humble, in the poor, in the sick, and in children."[16] Second, he proposes a perspective of inclusion, going beyond separation by opting for those who have been excluded and through a struggle for justice for them, by way of assistance that alleviates human suffering and systemic actions that reduce poverty. In the third place, he is relying on a multidimensional perspective, where on the margins the spiritual and socio-political converge, where evangelization meets humanization without false dichotomies. To satisfy one's hunger for bread is as important as satisfying one's hunger for companionship and for meaning. By moving toward the "margins," he shows a will to include all kinds of poverty, economic (material want), social (exclusion), psychological (loneliness), or cultural (rejection). Along with this multidimensionality of perspective on poverty, his concept of the margins makes allusion to the dynamisms that have been banished out to those margins, those who are at a distance from social power, those considered "forgettable," those whom society leaves out because they are superfluous, because they do not contribute to the logic of production or consumption, and indeed those who are outside the Church because of the Church. He breaks apart the category of those who give and those who receive, and in its place he puts instead the category of encounter in which we all give and receive, in which we learn "with the humble, the poor, the sick, and all those who are on the existential margins of life," all those who, in Pope Francis's words, "are the body of Christ."[17]

Why Not Turn to God for Inspiration?

Gustave Thibon stated that "one of the signs of mediocrity of spirit is to see contradictions where there are only contrasts (the fertile tension between different and complementary opposites)."[18] What is interesting about Pope Francis is how, in all his everyday encounters, though he says the same things to different people, he manages to create a kind of tension, a spark that varies from case to case, person to person.

The example comes to mind of what he said once during an audience with ambassadors from various countries.

> For her part, the Church always works for the integral development of every person. In this sense, she reiterates that the common good should not be simply an extra, simply a conceptual scheme of inferior quality tacked onto political programs. The Church encourages those in power to be truly at the service of the common good of their peoples. She urges financial leaders to take account of ethics and solidarity. And why should they not turn to God to draw inspiration from his designs? In this way, a new political and economic mindset would arise that would help to transform the

absolute dichotomy between the economic and social spheres into a healthy symbiosis.[19]

Francis's exhortation is indeed to transform the dichotomy between these two spheres into "healthy cooperation": he draws leaders into dialogue with their people, financial institutions into a consideration of an ethic of solidarity, allowing God to pose the question: "Why not turn to God for inspiration?" The most creative way of receiving Francis's words is listen to them when dichotomies appear and to be attentive to where he invites us to look, so that what at first seemed contradictory becomes instead a creative tension.

Peace Belongs to All Humanity

I might be so bold as to say that *on the political level*, by putting the subject of peace first and foremost, Francis has courageously shown the clear strategy that he has in mind and is gifted enough to show us the way forward. This he emphasized in an eloquent way when he proclaimed, at the Angelus on September 2013, a day of fasting and prayer for peace.

> Peace is a good that overcomes every barrier, because it belongs to all of humanity! I repeat forcefully: *it is neither a culture of confrontation nor a culture of conflict that builds harmony within and between peoples, but rather a culture of encounter and a culture of dialogue;* this is the only way to peace. May the plea for peace rise up and touch the heart of everyone so that they may lay down their weapons and let themselves be led by the

desire for peace.... Help us, Mary, to overcome this most difficult moment and to dedicate ourselves each day to building in every situation an authentic *culture of encounter and peace*. Mary, Queen of Peace, pray for us![20]

The Pope's insistence upon *dialogue* is interesting. He said to religious leaders,

> As leaders of different religions there is much we can do. Peace is the responsibility of everyone. To pray for peace, to work for peace! A religious leader is always a man or woman of peace, for the commandment of peace is inscribed in the depths of the religious traditions that we represent. But what can we do?[21]

His own insight on the practical level is: there is little peace because there is little dialogue; and during that period the Pope was in dialogue with everyone, from God to Putin, which showed in practice the importance of what he has said about dialogue. (And clearly he is sincere about it, as when he stated of his efforts to dialogue with the Argentinian government, "I didn't feel as if I had done everything possible; I felt that I could have been more insistent.")

> Peace requires a persistent, patient, strong, intelligent dialogue by which nothing is lost. Dialogue can overcome war. Dialogue can bring people of different generations who often ignore one another to live together; it makes citizens of different ethnic backgrounds and

makes people of different beliefs coexist. Dialogue is the way of peace. For dialogue fosters understanding, harmony, concord, and peace. For this reason, it is vital that it grow and expand between people of every condition and belief, like a net of peace that protects the world and especially protects the weakest members.[22]

By defining a leader as "someone in dialogue," he makes his classic distinction between intermediary and mediator:

Intermediaries seek to make concessions to everyone, so as to gain something for themselves. A mediator, instead, is someone who seeks nothing for himself but pours himself out for the process generously, until there is no more to give, knowing that the only thing to be gained is peace. Every one of us is called to be an artisan of peace, uniting and not dividing, eliminating hatred rather than holding on to it, opening pathways to dialogue and not raising the walls higher! Dialogue, meeting with one another to instill a culture of dialogue in the world, a culture of encounter.

His letter to Putin on September 4, 2013, is interesting because it is in synch with the goals of the meeting then going on among the G20, and in it he offers on a silver platter a way to address the issue:

Armed conflicts are always a deliberate negation of international harmony, and create profound divisions and deep wounds that require many years to heal. Wars are a concrete refusal to pursue the great economic and social goals that the international community has set for itself, as seen, for example, in the Millennium Development Goals."[23]

Money and the Disposal of Human Beings

The first pair of categories Francis contrasts is *politics and ethics*. To my mind, it's interesting to see the way he employs an ancient *midrash* to open our eyes to something that has become commonplace to our eyes.

In public life, in politics, if there is no ethics, an ethics of reference, everything is possible and everything can be done. We see, moreover, whenever we read the newspapers, that the lack of ethics in public life does great harm to the whole of humanity. I would like to tell you a story. I have already told it twice this week, but I will tell it a third time to you. It is taken from a biblical *midrash* by a twelfth-century rabbi. He tells the tale of the building of the Tower of Babel, and he says that, in order to build the Tower of Babel, bricks had to be made. What does this mean? Going out and mixing the mud, fetching straw, doing everything . . . then the kiln. And when the brick was made it had to be hoisted, for the construction of the Tower of Babel. Every brick was a treasure because of all the work required to make it. Whenever a brick fell, it was a national tragedy and the guilty workman was punished; a brick was so precious that if it fell there was a great drama. Yet if a workman fell, nothing happened, that was something else. This happens today: if the investments in the banks fall slightly . . . a tragedy . . . what can be done? But if people die of hunger, if they have nothing to eat, if they have poor health, it does not matter! This is our crisis today! And the witness of a poor Church for the poor goes against this mentality.[24]

That brick which is worth more than a human being is money, and this image makes concrete what might otherwise be just an abstraction, a category of thought, for indeed ethics speaks of that which "weighs" on the conscience because of its value.

Alongside the political dimension of peace, it is important to place economics as well. The Pope is quite direct about the most terrible consequence of the evil use of money: the disposal of human beings. The culture of encounter is endangered by a culture of disposal, and this illness arises from an anthropological reductionism that sees human beings, says the Pope, solely through the lens of what they consume.

> The worldwide *financial and economic* crisis seems to highlight their distortions and above all the gravely deficient human perspective, which reduces man to one of his needs alone, namely, consumption. Worse yet, human beings themselves are nowadays considered as consumer goods that can be used and thrown away. We have started a *throw-away culture*. This tendency is seen on the level of individuals and whole societies; and it is being promoted.[25]

According to Pope Francis, this problem is rooted in the relationship we have established with money:

One cause of this situation, in my opinion, is our *relationship with money*, and our acceptance of its power over ourselves and our society.... *Money has to serve, not to rule!* The Pope loves everyone, rich and poor alike, but the Pope has the duty, in Christ's name, to remind the rich to help the poor, to respect them, to promote them. The Pope appeals for disinterested solidarity and for a return to person-centered ethics in the world of finance and economics.[26]

The complete text of this discourse by the Pope has nothing superfluous in it, so it is not easy to give a mere summary. At first glance, it presents the social doctrine of the Church, which all Popes espouse, and yet his words strike deep in the heart and the mind. "Money should of service to us, rather than rule over us." Here is one of Francis's proverbial sayings that goes deep. Why? Simply because of its originality? No, there is more to it than that. Such sayings strike deeply because they come from someone who has always acted to ensure that money serves the poor. They strike deeply because, as he speaks, he acts accordingly: for example, he forgoes the use of a luxury car; he pays his own rent; he has gone about reforming the management of the Vatican's finances; he has suspended the bishop who has scandalized the faithful with his exorbitant spending; he has insisted that religious orders turn their empty houses into hostels rather than make them over into profitable hotels.

Francis has integrity on every level: doctrinal, practical, personal, ecclesiastical, and social. His attitude toward money has always been "put it to use"—spread it around!, as his venerated Blessed Artémides Zatti[27] would say. And because we see his words on this topic effecting spontaneous change in so many people in such a brief period of time, representing "a breath of fresh air" in the Church and throughout the world, his thoughts and deeds about money ought well to spur our own reflection.

Social Inclusion

The Pope's vision of society is inclusive, a theme that he speaks about all the time, and in particular when he talks about young people.[28]

> Our youth today is in crisis. We all are used to this culture of disposal; with the elderly, it has become all too common. But we practice it as well with a large number of young people who are unemployed: they too are suffering from this culture of disposal. We need to change this habit we have of throwing things away. No! *A culture of inclusion*, a culture of encounter, making an effort to *include everyone* in society. This is what I want to communicate in my visit to these young people, these young people in society.[29]

Inclusion implies an effort to accept difference, to dialogue with those who think differently,[30] to support the participation of those with different abilities.[31] "We must never allow the throwaway culture to enter our hearts, because we are brothers and sisters. No one is disposable!"[32] In his talk at the FAO, the Pope emphasized that the year

2014 should be dedicated to rural families. To promote a culture of encounter and solidarity requires that one promote "a spirit of true fraternity to our world, enabling it to feel as a single family, where the greatest attention is paid to those most in need."[33] In his statement on World Refugee Day, he insisted that we must make ours a culture of encounter and of welcome, and not a culture of rejection and refusal. The image the Church offers here is basic, that of a

> People of God that embraces all peoples and brings to them the proclamation of the Gospel, for the face of each person bears the mark of the face of Christ! Here we find the deepest foundation of the dignity of the human person, which must always be respected and safeguarded. It is less the criteria of efficiency, productivity, social class, or ethnic or religious belonging that ground that personal dignity so much as the fact of being created in God's own image and likeness (see Gen 1:26-27) and, even more so, being children of God. Every human being is a child of God![34]

This perspective alone is what leads us to see in the immigrant or the refugee not simply an issue to deal with but a brother or a sister who needs welcoming, respect, and love.

> A change of attitude towards migrants and refugees is needed on the part of everyone, moving away from attitudes of defensiveness and fear, indifference and

marginalization—all typical of a throwaway culture—
toward attitudes based on a culture of encounter, the
only culture capable of building a better, more just, and
fraternal world. The communications media are themselves called to embrace this "conversion of attitudes"
and to promote this change in the way migrants and
refugees are treated.[35]

With reference to his own country, Argentina, his video
message on the feast of San Gaetano was significant. This
observance was one of his favorite times to encounter the
faithful, walking on foot and greeting people one by one.[36]

> What Jesus teaches us first of all is to meet one another,
> and in meeting to offer one another help. We must
> know how to meet one another. We must build, create,
> construct a culture of encounter. How many differ-
> ences, how many problems in the family there always
> are! Problems in the neighborhood, problems at work,
> problems everywhere. And differences don't help. The
> culture of encounter. Going out to meet one another.[37]

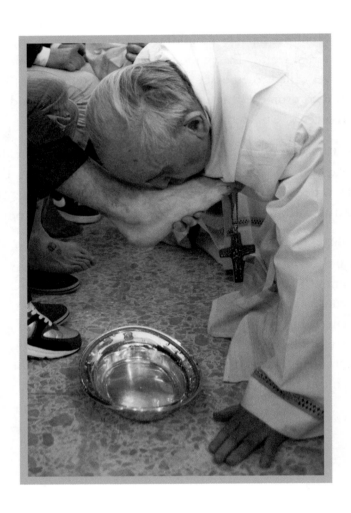

SIX

The New Ministry
of Relationship

THE MINISTRY OF THE CHURCH begins with proclamation and witness. Working among the people through charitable works, by way of personal exchange and dialogue, we build up a culture of encounter. As is his habit, the Pope draws attention to three things, emphasizing that we ought to be "nearly obsessed" with our mission to serve a culture of encounter. He expresses a certainty. He makes a request. And he gives us a task.

The certainty is that of someone, happy and humble, who has been found and who, therefore, can move toward an encounter with others with conviction.

> Have the courage to go against the tide of this culture of efficiency, this culture of waste. Encountering and welcoming everyone, solidarity—a word that is being hidden by this culture, as if it were a bad word—solidarity and fraternity: these are what make our society truly human. Be servants of communion and of the culture of encounter! I would like you to be almost obsessed about this. Be so without being presumptuous, imposing "our truths," but rather be guided by the humble yet joyful certainty of

those who have been found, touched, and transformed by the Truth who is Christ, ever to be proclaimed."[1]

We must pray that the Virgin Mary lead us to go out of ourselves. The way the Pope says this is quite beautiful:

The Virgin Mary is our exemplar.... Let us ask her to teach us to encounter one another in Jesus every day. And when we pretend not to notice because we have many things to do and the tabernacle is abandoned, may she take us by the hand. Let us ask this of her! Watch over me, Mother, when I am disoriented, and lead me by the hand. May you spur us on to meet our many brothers and sisters who are on the outskirts, who are hungry for God but have no one to proclaim him. May you not force us out of our homes, but encourage us to go out so that we may be disciples of the Lord. May you grant all of us this grace.[2]

Setting aside any form of ministry that keeps people at a distance, our task consists of acting to bring light and sunshine to every heart.

At Aparecida, two categories of ministry were emphasized, both of which arise from the same place in the Gospel and are useful as criteria to evaluate how well we are living out our mission as disciples: closeness and encounter. Neither of these is new, but they both are the ways in which God revealed Himself in history. He is a God "close to his people," and the greatest manifestation of His closeness to us is His incarnation. This is a God who goes out and encounters His people. In Latin America and in the Caribbean, there are ministries carried out "at a distance," in accordance with organizational principles and procedures, obviously without any sense of closeness, tenderness, or touch. In such places, the "tender revolution" wrought by the Incarnation of the Word is not known. Ministries done at arm's length cannot experience an encounter, an encounter with Jesus Christ, an encounter with one's brothers; and from such efforts, the most one can hope for is a sort of proselytizing; but even then, never do they actually succeed in establishing a church. Closeness is what creates communion and belonging; it makes encounter possible. Closeness enables dialogue and creates a culture of encounter. One touchstone for judging closeness and the capacity for encounter of a particular ministry is the homily. How are our homilies? Do we follow closely the example of our Lord who spoke "as one who has authority" or do we merely make distant and abstract observations?

And the Pope charges his bishops with looking after the people, "above all instilling hope: so that light will shine in people's hearts."[3]

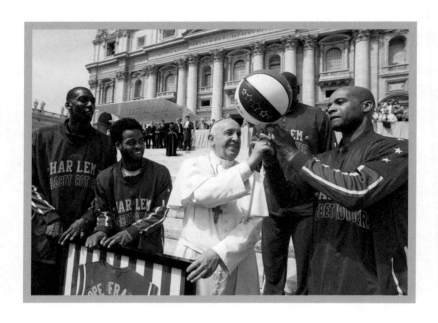

SEVEN

A New Culture in the Church

To REFLECT ON a culture of encounter in the thought of Pope Francis means to make a distinction (*indivise et inconfuse*, "with neither division nor confusion") between beauty, goodness, and truth, with an emphasis on truth. This distinction, when applied to Francis, corresponds to what he communicates through his actions and gestures (waving, smiling, placing his hands on the sick, *mate* in the midst of the crowd, bringing his rosary to his ears); through what he expresses by his tasks, choices, decisions, preferences; and what he expresses by way of his *logos*, thought, spoken words. By making use of his whole being and person so as to be able to dialogue in a clear and responsible way brings into focus the other two transcendent realities (goodness and beauty) and makes them "concrete universals," as he is fond of saying. His thought is neither abstract–universal nor concrete–particular.

From this perspective, we might characterize his thoughts on the culture of encounter with three words (two of which are actually images).

His is a kind of "church-bell thought," one of those great bells that calls everyone together, simple in the way it rings out a complex polyphonic chord. It is a way of thinking that creates a culture of encounter, because its ringing invites everyone—as a church bell does—to dialogue, calling us all with its sound to an encounter with one another.

Francis's way of thinking is also a kind of "shoe-leather thought," and here one thinks of his own worn black shoes during his ministry on the streets of Buenos Aires. His is a way of thinking that "walks the walk," a phenomenological "path" that moves toward encounter as a companion, through the mud, in pilgrimage with his people, standing in line. In this sense his is a thought that shapes a culture and leaves its footprint on the course of time—the very opposite of any kind of magical, gnostic, or enlightened way of thinking.

And finally, his thought is "friendly." On every level, he gives us his friendship, in his camaraderie (as "one of Jesus's company," to be sure, a Jesuit); in brotherhood (as his name Francis indicates); in his "predilection" (through what he has chosen in discernment, the highest common good for the greater glory of God).

In all these ways, his thought, which expresses so creatively what a "culture of encounter" can be, looks on all of us with love, thereby bringing such a culture into being and making us the recipients of its fruit.

Study Guide

CHAPTER ONE

For reflection and sharing

Francis says, "Ask yourselves this question: How often is Jesus inside and knocking at the door to be let out, to come out? And we do not let him out because of our own need for security, because so often we are locked into ephemeral structures that serve solely to make us slaves and not free children of God."

Meditate today on the ways in which you have felt the prompting of Jesus to go beyond what feels familiar and safe. Where has Jesus been calling you to go beyond your comfort zone?

For prayer and practice

"In this 'stepping out' it is important to be ready for encounter. For me this word is very important. Encounter with others. Why? Because faith is an encounter with Jesus, and we must do what Jesus does: encounter others."

Commit today to greet with love and goodwill three people whom you might not otherwise.

CHAPTER TWO

For reflection and sharing

Francis says that "prayer touches our heart." Take some quiet time to focus in on your heart, your center. Who or what has touched it recently?

For prayer and practice

"This is what Pope Francis is encouraging when, for example, he speaks of charitable giving, a gesture that is only an authentic encounter when we look into the eyes of the person we are helping, touching his hands, exchanging words. 'If I simply toss him some coins . . . if I have not actually touched him, I have not encountered him.'"

Commit today to what our Pope describes as an authentic encounter: looking into the eyes of someone who needs your help and physically touching that person in some way.

CHAPTER THREE

For reflection and sharing

"The incarnation of the Gospel demands that Christ be proclaimed and welcomed in different ways in different countries and in different environments, acknowledging the richness in each of them."

Bring to prayer today the variety of ways in your everyday life you have encountered cultural differences, reflecting on how these have challenged you spiritually or giving thanks for the ways in which these differences have enriched your life.

For prayer and practice

Francis says, "All peoples have a voice, even if it has been reduced by oppression to a whisper. We must sharpen our hearing and listen to that voice, and not speak in their place."

Commit today to taking time to listen to someone whom you might not otherwise pay attention to: a neighbor, a family member, a stranger in line in front of you at the store, the homeless person at the bus stop. What kind of voice do they have? And what did you hear?

CHAPTER FOUR

For reflection and sharing

Consolation is a key notion in the spirituality of St. Ignatius, and it is the experience of God's presence in us and around us. As the author writes, "When a work has been done for God, with dedication and love, patiently kneaded into the monotony of one's daily routine, when the grace of consolation finally comes, it shines in all its splendor."

In your prayer today, lift up with thanks those moments of consolation, God's presence, that you have experienced in the past few weeks, and let your focus be on how this consolation feels within you, spiritually and physically.

For prayer and practice

Select three everyday tasks that you need to accomplish today, and before each, take a moment to dedicate your action to God out of love, gratitude, or praise. How does that transform this action for you?

Chapter Five

For reflection and sharing

The author speaks of Japanese bamboo which, after many years, shows amazing and unexpected growth. In your prayer today, reflect on the ways you or someone you love has grown spiritually in ways you might not have anticipated or expected. Take time in prayer to give thanks for this growth. Then, pray some on ways you would like to experience growth in your own life and open yourself spiritually to God's nourishment and help in this area.

For prayer and practice

Francis uses the image of music to capture the movement of the Holy Spirit in our lives. Take time today to listen to a piece of music that you find inspiring, comforting, or spiritually uplifting.

CHAPTER SIX

For reflection and sharing

The Pope encourages us to turn to Mary and gives us this prayer for the day:

> Watch over me, Mother, when I am disoriented, and lead me by the hand. May you spur us on to meet our many brothers and sisters who are on the outskirts, who are hungry for God but have no one to proclaim him. May you not force us out of our homes, but encourage us to go out so that we may be disciples of the Lord. May you grant all of us this grace.

Take three moments throughout the day to pray this prayer, keeping in mind those places where we need guidance, where we are challenged to be generous to others, or where we might be a faithful witness to Jesus before others.

For prayer and practice

Pope Francis contrasts a culture of encounter with a culture of waste. Each of us finds ourselves challenged both spiritually and materially to appreciate God's creation fully by avoiding unnecessary consumption or spending. Take a moment to consider one way you might forgo an unneeded expenditure and then do so, just for today. Reflect on how it feels to consciously and deliberate set limits on your desires or pleasures.

CHAPTER SEVEN

For reflection and sharing

It can be a challenge to pray without words, but the image of a church bell here is a good one to direct oneself toward a different and more meditative form of prayer. Quiet yourself down, light a candle and take a moment to ring a bell, focusing, as best you can without words, on letting this sound be your prayer as it fades into silence.

For prayer and practice

The image of Francis's shoe-leather theology, which walks the walk, challenges us to pray in yet another way: by walking. Take five minutes to do a walking meditation today, slowly and deliberately paying attention to the way your body moves as you walk in prayer.

Notes

CHAPTER ONE

1. See 1 Corinthians 12:7.
2. Pope Francis, *Vigil of Pentecost with the Ecclesial Movements*, May 18, 2013 (italics mine).
3. Shelter for the homeless in which Fr. Diego Fares worked.
4. Alfonso López Quintás was a Spanish philosopher and teacher, born in 1928.
5. R. Guardini, *El contraste* (Madrid: Biblioteca de Autores Cristianos, 1996), 57; Italian translation: *L'opposizione polare* (Brescia: Morcelliana, 1997).
6. José Gabriel del Rosario Brochero (1840–1914), a saintly Argentinean Catholic priest, was beatified September 14, 2013.

CHAPTER TWO

1. In 1986, Fr. Jorge Bergoglio went to Germany to complete his doctoral thesis on Romano Guardini.
2. R. Guardini, *Libertad, gracia y destino* (Buenos Aires: Lumen, 1994), 40; Italian translation, *Libertá, grazia, destino* (Brescia: Morcelliana, 2009). Guardini has in mind Paul's encounter with Jesus, whose grace made him fall to the ground and blinded him, touching his heart.
3. J. M. Bergoglio, *Reflexiones en esperanza* (Buenos Aires: USAL, 1992), 16.

4. Ibid., 15.

5. Ibid., 40ff.

6. R. Guardini., *La existencia del cristiano* (Madrid: BAC, 1997), 459; Italian translation, *L'esistenza del cristiano* (Milan: Vita e Pensiero, 1985). "Equally crucial for a person's health is love. . . . One may grow ill, but one never gives up on love. Even when a man lacks it, it can wound him, even when he falls into egotism and hatred, even when he dismisses it as frivolous and founds his life on manipulation, force, or cleverness. That is when his existence becomes a prison. All is closed off. Things oppress us, everything becomes foreign and inimical in the most intimate way, our final, clear meaning disappears. Life does not grow" (ibid.). "A person grows ill when he gives up on justice. Not when he commits an injustice, but when he gives up on justice itself. Justice means recognizing that things possess an essentiality that disposes one to preserve the right of things and the order which is derived from that right" (R. Guardini, *Mundo y persona* (Madrid: Encuentro, 107ff.; Italian translation, *Mondo e persona* (Brescia: Morcelliana, 2007).

7. R. Guardini, *Begegnung und Bildung* (Würzberg: Werkbund, 1956), 20. "Man has no consistency when he lives in himself and for himself, but when he is 'open,' when he ventures out toward what is other, especially toward the other . . . to give oneself over to something that is worth risking losing oneself by going in such a direction."

8. R. Guardini, *Ética: Lecciones en la Universidad de Múnich* (Madrid: BAC, 2000), 190; Italian translation: *Etica* (Brescia: Morcelliana, 2003).

9. Earlier, he described Jesus as one with an extraordinary "authority," *exousia*, a power that comes from his very being. "A Jesus who in fact strikes, divides, innovates—he himself says so—because of his relationship to God, whom he familiarly

calls 'Abba,' who has given him this 'authority,' so that he may use it for the good of mankind."

10. Francis, *Letter to Journalist Eugenio Scalfari*, September 11, 2013.

CHAPTER THREE

1. J. M. Bergoglio, *Meditaciones para religiosos* (San Miguel: Diego de Torres, 1982), 46. This and the quotations that follow are from this work.

2. A major Marian shrine in Argentina and popular place of pilgrimage.

3. Another place of pilgrimage.

4. Bergoglio, *Meditaciones para religiosos*, 46.

5. Ibid., 47.

6. Ibid.

7. Paul VI, *Evangelii nuntiandi*. Cf. J. M. Bergoglio, *Memorial público a los padres de la comunidad del CIAS* (1977), n. 23.

8. For this passage, see J. M. Bergoglio, *Reflexiones espirituales* (San Miguel: Diego de Torres, 1987), 285ff.

9. Ibid. Cf. Decrees of the 32rd General Congregation of the Society of Jesus (1977), 4.54.

10. Bergoglio, *Reflexiones espirituales,* 309ff.

11. Ibid. Cf. Decrees of the 32rd General Congregation of the Society of Jesus (1977), n. 50.

12. Bergoglio, *Reflexiones en esperanza*, 273-99.

13. Ibid, 286.

14. Ibid., 290. Cf. R. Guardini, *El ocaso de la edad moderna* (Madrid: Cristianidad, 1981), 122; Italian translation: *La fine dell'epoca moderna* (Brescia: Morcelliana, 1993).

15. Bergoglio, *Reflexiones en esperanza*, 297.

16. Ibid., 298.

17. Ibid., 293 n. 30.

18. Ibid., 298ff.

19. Jorge Bergoglio, *El verdadero poder es el servicio* (Buenos Aires: Claretiana, 2007), 88.

20. President of the Pontifical Catholic University of Argentina.

21. V. M. Fernandez, *Interview*, "Clarin," October 27, 2013.

Chapter Four

1. Without overlooking Erich Przywara and his notion of an ever-greater God and of a Spirit that moves everything and creates harmony from diversity; along with Hans Urs von Balthasar and his ordering of transcendentals, which places Beauty and Goodness (always dramatic) before Logic; and his way of opening every finite, philosophical truth to Christ (to direct every truth toward Christ) and his art of clarifying transposition (which brings unity to multiplicity; which translates the one Word into many, under a loving, creative, and merciful eye.

2. J. M. Bergoglio, *Educar en la cultura del encuentro*, September 1, 1999.

3. This formula became more and more important, and Bergoglio used it again at Luján and on Christmas. On those occasions, he centered the culture of encounter around Mary, whose "gaze pushes us forward to weave a culture of encounter" (homily at Luján); and around St. Joseph, "in whose closeness and encounter Jesus was born and lived" (homily on Christmas).

4. Bergoglio, *Educar en la cultura del encuentro*.

5. Ibid.

6. 1 Corinthians 12:10.

7. Near the Marian shrine of Aparecida, the popular shrine in Brazil, in 2007, the last general assembly of CELAM took place, that is, the assembly of Latin American bishops; Bergoglio, at that time Cardinal, directed the revision of the final document.

8. "From the encounter between this faith and the indigenous people was born the rich Christian culture of our continent." "For Latin American and Caribbean countries to accept the Christian faith meant to know and welcome Christect. . . . Authentic cultures are not closed in on themselves . . . but are open. Even more, they seek out encounter with other cultures, because only truth unites, and the proof of this is love" (Benedict XVI, Inaugural Address). Cf. Aparecida 13. In our lands there has occurred a "dramatic and unequal encounter of peoples and cultures," the synthesis of which can be found in Our Lady of Guadalupe. Even in our country Mary leads us to encounter one other in our differences (J. M. Bergoglio, *Propuestas de Aparecida para la pastoral de la Iglesia en Argentina*, June 15, 2009; the following two quotations are from this document).

9. J. M. Bergoglio, *Conferencia en la XII Jornada de Pastoral Social*, September 19, 2009.

10. Bergoglio, *Conferencia en la XIII Jornada de Pastoral Social, Hacia un Bicentenario en Justicia y Solidaridad 2010–2016. Nosotros como ciudadanos, nosotros como pueblo*, October 16, 2010.

CHAPTER FIVE

1. J. M. Bergoglio, *Homily at the Closing Mass of the Meeting of Urban Ministry in the Buenos Aires Region*, September 2, 2012.

2. Cf. J. M. Bergoglio, "El sentido teológico de la elección," *Boletin de espiritualidad* 1 (1968), 3, 7-8. One year before his ordination, in his first article published in the recently begun *Boletin de espiritualidad*, Bergoglio, in two brief pages, reflected upon the "theological meaning of the election." Here already is the image, which he coined, of the Lord "who has chosen us to be first," who goes before us with his grace.

3. We recall here how, in 1975, it happened that young people were surprised by the provincial the Jesuits of Mendoza had chosen for themselves; and yet, as young as he was, he led with authority. In a short time, he assigned over twenty Jesuits to the missionary group and sent them out to the poorest areas of the country.

4. The International Congress of Theology on "The Evangelization of Culture and the Inculturation of Faith" in 1985 brought together specialists from all over the world at the Collegio Massimo along with a local mission in the parish neighborhood where around ten student Jesuits were working.

5. Monsignor Victor Manuel Fernández, who worked side by side with the Cardinal to provide the Assembly daily copies of the fruit of their labors, described it in this way: "It was quite a sight watching him move about at Aparecida, seeing his capacity to create consensus, to set the tone, to inspire trust. For me, who am an anxious sort of person, his patience and his capacity to seize the opportune moment were really striking. This is when I saw his conviction that, rather than obtain immediate results, one needs to put into motion a process. As for the Aparecida document, he didn't worry about its being impeccably edited but cared more that it would be a synthesis of spirituality and social/missionary ministry. One thing that he was concerned about was popular piety, because he was worried that the Church didn't properly appreciate the faith and

the values of the poor" (V. W. Fernández, *Interview*, "Clarin," October 27, 2013).

6. The two ex-presidents of Argentina who fought with each other and reconciled.

7. Francis, *Vigil of Pentecost*.

8. Cf. J. M. Bergoglio, *Homily at the Mass with the Bishops at the 28th GMG*, San Sebastiano Cathedral, Rio de Janeiro, July 27, 2013. "We help young people. We lend our ear to listen to their dreams—they need to be listened to—to hear of their successes, to hear of their difficulties. We need to sit down. Maybe we are hearing the same libretto but *with different music*, with a different identity. Have the patience to listen! I am asking this of you from the bottom of my heart. In confession, in spiritual direction, in companionship. We need to know how to spend time with them" (italics mine).

9. J. García Roca, "La narrativa cordial del cristianismo. El magisterio del Papa Francisco," *Iglesia viva* 48 (2013), 41, 42.

10. Ibid.

11. Francis, *Letter to the Journalist Eugenio Scalfari*.

12. Francis, *Vigil of Pentecost* (italics mine).

13. St. Albert Hurtado, at the end of his life, wanted to write a book on the "sense of poverty." He wrote to his friend Arturo Gaete, "If you are worried about my health, please know that I am much better after a month of rest in the port [of Valparaiso]. I hope to write this summer (or begin writing) on the sense of poverty. I believe that is the core of Christianity, and every time there is greater resistance and a lack of understanding toward everything that expresses poverty" ("Letter to Arturo Gaete," Santiago, Chile, January 1952, in *Cartas e informes*, 315-16).

14. Bergoglio, *Reflexiones en esperanza*, 30-33.

15. J. M. Bergoglio, *El tesoro de nuesto barro: Homilía en la fiesta de San Pio X*, August 21, 2003. "Only the person who

knows he is vulnerable is capable of acting in solidarity. To be moved by (move alongside), to feel compassion for (suffer with) whoever is on the margins is the attitude of one who is capable of seeing himself in another, a mixture of dirt and treasure, and thus does not reject the other. Rather, he loves the other, he draws close to that image and without realizing it finds that the woundedness he is healing in the other are his own wounds. Compassion is transformed into communion, through a connection that brings closeness and bonding. Neither criminals nor those who take advantage of the weak know the treasure they hold nor the dirt they carry within. For that reason the former feel no reverence for the lives of others and leave them for dead. If they do not value their own lives, how could they possibly value the lives of others? Those who exploit others, on the other hand, give great value to their own lives but in an imperfect way: they only see one part of themselves, that which they hold dear. They feel chosen, the elect of God (usually in an ostentatious way, as in the parables of Jesus when he describes two religious characters of his time, a Levite and a Pharisee), but they lack the courage to acknowledge that they are clay, fragile mud. For these people, whoever has failed frightens them, and they do not know how to recognize them. How can one know another's dirt if one does not accept one's own?"

16. This is a quote from *Address to the Participants of the Plenary Assembly of the International Union of Superiors General,* which the Pope gave on May 8, 2013.

17. J. García Roca. "La narrative cordial del cristianismo. El magisterio del Papa Francisco," 43-46. The subsequent quotations from the Pope are from the *Visit to the "Astalli Center," Jesuit Refugee Service in Rome,* September 10, 2013.

18. G. Thibon, *El pan de cada dia* (Madrid: Rialp, 1952), 63,

quoted by A. López Quintás, in *El contraste* (Madrid: BAC, 1996), 11.

19. Francis, *Address to the New Non-Resident Ambassadors to the Holy See*, May 26, 2013.

20. Francis, *Angelus*, September 1, 2013.

21. Francis, *Address to the Participants in the International Meeting for Peace*, September 30, 2013.

22. Ibid.

23. Francis, *Letter to H. E. Mr. Vladimir Putin, President of the Russian Federation on the Occasion of the G20 Summit in St. Petersburg*, September 4, 2013. The Millennium Development Goals (MDG) of the United Nations are goals related to poverty and to the socio-economic development of all the member states of the United Nations which are targeted to be reached by the year 2015.

24. Francis, *Vigil of Pentecost*.

25. *Address to the New Non-Resident Ambassadors*.

26. Ibid.

27. Artémides Zatti (1880–1951), Salesian brother from Italy who ministered to the poor in Patagonia. He was beatified April 14, 2002.

28. Inclusion is a central theme for Francis and always has been: "The inclusion or the exclusion of those who are wounded by the side of the road defines every economic, political, social, and religious project" (*Te Deum*, May 25, 2003). Thus, "one must be quite audacious to go against the tide, to refrain from giving up on whatever utopia might be possible to realize, for inclusion has been both the style and the rhythm of our past. To walk forward as a people together is always a slower walk" (*Letter to Catechists*, August 21, 2004). At Aparecida, Francis noted that "to move toward a life-giving

encounter is characterized by inclusion over any form of exclusion" (see Aparecida 8.3; preferential option for the poor and excluded). Jesus challenges exclusion as part of a worthy life because "those excluded are not simply 'exploited' but 'superfluous' and 'have nothing to lose.' Inclusion welcomes, it brings us close, we enter by it into the 'dynamic of the Good Samaritan' through 'closeness'" (*The Aparecida Proposal for the Clergy of the Church in Argentina*, June 15, 2009). "For this reason, we are preparing the Eucharist while walking, as a sign of inclusion, making space for all to come in, moving out toward the margins of life. In this society of so many exclusive places, so many circles of power, we would like to make for the Lord a 'great hall' of this plaza, in which there is a place for everyone. This way all may be seated around the Lord's table, at a celebration in which this hall, which many who have been invited have looked down upon, might be filled with humble guests who want to take joyful part in the gracious action of the Lord" (Homily of Corpus Domini, June 12, 2012).

29. To journalists on his flight to Rio de Janeiro, July 22, 2013.

30. Here a previously quoted text is worth repeating: "We live in a culture of conflict, a culture of fragmentation, a culture in which I throw away what is of no use to me, a culture of waste. Yet on this point, I ask you to think—and it is part of the crisis—of the elderly, who are the wisdom of a people, think of the children . . . the culture of waste! However, we must go out to meet them, and with our faith we must create a 'culture of encounter,' a culture of friendship, a culture in which we find brothers and sisters, in which we can also speak with those who think differently, as well as those who hold other beliefs, who do not have the same faith. They all have something in

common with us: they are images of God, they are children of God. Going out to meet everyone, without losing sight of our own position."

31. Cf. Francis, *Discourse to the Unseen*, June 13, 2013.

32. *Visit to the Community of Varginha*, July 25, 2013.

33. *Address to the Participants in the 38th Conference of the Food and Agriculture Organization of the United Nations (FAO)*, June 20, 2013.

34. *Message for the World Day of Migrants and Refugees*, August 5, 2013.

35. Ibid.

36. Saint Cajetan of Thiene was a very popular saint in Argentina, venerated particularly by workers as the patron of bread and of work. On his feast day, August 7, the faithful in Buenos Aires would form a long line to kiss the window of the reliquary that held the small statue of the saint.

37. *Video Message on the Occasion of the Feast of Saint Cajetan*, August 7, 2013.

CHAPTER SIX

1. *Mass with Bishops, Priests, Religious, and Seminarians*, July 27, 2013.

2. Ibid.

3. *Address to the Leadership of the Episcopal Conferences of Latin America (CELAM)*, July 28, 2013.

Photo Credits

About the Author

DIEGO FARES, S.J., is a Jesuit priest from Argentina. He is professor of philosophy and theology, and director of "El hogar de San Jose," a home for the elderly living in the streets or in extreme poverty. He has known and worked with Jorge Bergoglio for over forty years.

About the Translator

ROBERT H. HOPCKE is the author of numerous works in the field of Jungian psychology and Roman Catholic spirituality. He has translated a variety of books in fields as diverse as art history, sexuality and religion, including most recently, with Paul A. Schwartz, *The Little Flowers of St. Francis*, from Shambhala Publications.

About the Publisher

The CROSSROAD PUBLISHING COMPANY publishes CROSSROAD and HERDER & HERDER books. We offer a 200-year global family tradition of books on spiritual living and religious thought. We promote reading as a time-tested discipline for focus and understanding. We help authors shape, clarify, write, and effectively promote their ideas. We select, edit, and distribute books. With our expertise and passion we provide wholesome spiritual nourishment for heart, mind, and soul through the written word.

The Pope Francis Resource Library

In these unique volumes that aim to give deeper insight into the spirituality and theology of Pope Francis, you will find carefully selected texts from works by Archbishop Bergoglio (exclusively published in English by Crossroad), and texts by Pope Francis (authorized by the Vatican for these editions).

POPE FRANCIS
Jorge Mario Bergoglio

Open Mind, Faithful Heart

Reflections on Following Jesus

Introduction by Gustavo Larrazábal CFM
Prologue by José María Arancedo, Archbishop
of Santa Fe de la Vera Cruz

ISBN 978-0-8245-2085-4
$24.95 pb / 320 pages

ISBN 978-0-8245-1997-1
$29.95 hc / 320 pages

E-book editions available

The Crossroad Publishing Company

OPEN MIND, FAITHFUL HEART
Reflections on Following Jesus

This book is not just for reading. It is a path for prayer and a guide for life.

Pope Francis connects with people, especially the young, the forgotten, and the forlorn. The cameras show him in Rome, in Brazil, in Lampedusa reaching out to the crowds, holding infants, embracing the disabled.

What is the source of his energy and his spiritual vitality? This book is perhaps the best introduction to what makes the Pope the engaging pastor he is.

During his years as archbishop of Buenos Aires, Jorge Bergoglio often spoke to those collaborating with him in pastoral ministry. His constant theme was how to follow Jesus unreservedly, even in the hectic turmoil of our modern world. The texts of these talks, handpicked by the author for this volume, reveal the spiritual depths of Pope Francis as perhaps no other work does. The strong scriptural orientation of the Pope is evident in the countless references to both Old and New Testaments. To help the reader, this edition has supplemented the original text with appropriate scriptural citations.

The language of these pages speaks to the heart as much as to the mind. These are meditations to be savored rather than just read quickly and filed away.

> "The secret of
> Pope Francis is found
> in this book."
> —Bishop Martinez Camino

The Crossroad Publishing Company

OPEN MIND, FAITHFUL HEART
Reflections on Following Jesus

"In a sea of books by, for, and about Pope Francis, this outstanding (and particularly attractive) volume by the Argentine Pontiff HIMSELF takes us inside his mind, heart, and soul and gives us a blueprint for living, an example of how to live the Christian vocation. I highly recommend it!"
>   —Deacon James Keating, Ph.D., Institute for Priestly Formation, Creighton University

"I highly recommend this volume as instructive and illuminating spiritual reading for all audiences."
>   —Rev. Thomas Massaro, S.J.

"I finished this book feeling that I knew Pope Francis better. The media may not find in this collection of essays the one-liners that are heard so often. But anyone who delves into this book will come away knowing that, indeed, the world has a pope with truly an open mind and a faithful heart."
>   —Deacon Michael E. Bulson, St. Andrew Parish, Riverton, Utah

"Christians of any denomination will find this book by the reigning pontiff to be of great assistance in their personal spiritual journey. Intentionally composed to be useful in ordinary day-to-day situations, the monograph will be highly useful for individual prayer and meditation as well as serviceable to prayer and Bible study groups."
>   —Fr. Rick Gribble, C.S.C.

"To read this volume is to get a strong sense of Francis's own sense of mission and the way he is trying to offer his own path as a guide for others."
>   —Christopher M. Bellitto, Ph.D., author of
>   *101 Questions and Answers on Popes and the Papacy*

The Crossroad Publishing Company

Excerpts from *Open Mind, Faithful Heart*

"We will never be able to explain to our complete satisfaction the mysterious designs of God, who has wanted to reveal himself in the course of history. Over a long stretch of time we humans have been learning, like little children from their father, how to recognize and respond to the face of God. None of the Lord's past revelations was partial; they all mysteriously contained the totality of the mystery of God in Christ; we perceived it only slowly, in bits and pieces. It is the same with our personal histories: the Lord reveals himself 'historically' in the unfathomable mystery of those who seek God and also in those who reject God and flee from him. That is to say, God reveals himself in the historical mystery of our movement through grace and sin."

"To engage effectively in any struggle, one must be fully confident of victory. Those who begin a struggle without robust confidence have already lost half the battle. Christian victory always involves a cross, but a cross that is the banner of victory. We can learn about militant faith and nourish it in ourselves by moving among the poor. During these meditations, we will remember the faces of many people whom we have known in our past pastoral labors. Those faces of the humble folk with their simple piety are always faces of triumph, but they are also almost always accompanied by the cross. In contrast, the faces of the arrogant are always faces of defeat. They do not accept the cross; they want an easy resurrection. They separate what God has united. They want to be like God. The spirit of defeat entices us to commit ourselves to losing causes. It knows nothing of the powerful tenderness that can be seen in the seriousness with which a child blesses himself or in the profundity with which an elderly woman says her prayers. That is faith, and that is the best vaccine against the spirit of defeat."

 The Crossroad Publishing Company

Excerpts from *Open Mind, Faithful Heart*

"Rather than being a distant deity, God is the Father who accompanies all growth; he is the daily bread that nourishes; he is the merciful one who is near at hand in the moments when the enemy would exploit his children. God is the Father who gives his children what they request if it is appropriate; but whether he grants it or not, he is always affectionate toward them. If we accept the reality that God expresses himself within our human limits, then we should also accept the limits of our own pastoral expression. Our honest limitations distance us from the ideas of those who think they have the key to the world, those who know nothing of waiting patiently and working hard, and those who are easily swayed by hysteria and illusion."

"Another temptation is to prefer head-values to heart-values. That should not be the case. Only the heart unifies and integrates. Intellect without a sense of piety tends to divide. The heart unites ideas with reality, time with space, life with death and with eternity. The temptation is to dislodge intellect from the place where God our Lord put it. He gave it to us so that we could clarify faith. God did not create human intelligence so that we could set ourselves up as judges of all things. It is a light that has only been lent to us, a mere reflection. Our intellect is not the light of the world; it is simply a flash for illuminating our faith."

The Crossroad Publishing Company

The Pope Francis Resource Library

The People Wish to See Jesus

Reflections for Those Who Teach

Written with expressive gratitude for the work of teachers, and translated exclusively for this volume from talks by Archbishop Bergoglio for the catechists of Buenos Aires, offering deep understanding and challenge for successful catechesis, teaching, and education.

ISBN 978-0-8245-2036-6

$19.95 pb / 140 pages

Please support your local bookstore or order directly from the publisher at www.crossroadpublishing.com.

To request a catalog or inquire about quantity orders, please email sales@crossroadpublishing.com

The Crossroad Publishing Company

THE POPE FRANCIS RESOURCE LIBRARY

Stefan von Kempis and Philip F. Lawler (editors)

A Call to Serve

Pope Francis and the Catholic Future

This thoughtful, vivid introduction to Pope Francis's life and his promising future in the Vatican details the historic events surrounding Pope Benedict XVI's resignation, the subsequent election of Pope Francis, and the particulars of the new Pope's spirituality and thought.

ISBN 978-0-8245-5005-9

$16.95 pb / 160 pages

2014
Eric Hoffer Award
FINALIST
Excellence in
Independent
Publishing

The Crossroad Publishing Company